The Power *Of* Meditation

Prayer Journal Hindu Edition

Activinotes

Activinotes
DAILY JOURNALS, PLANNERS, NOTEBOOKS AND OTHER BLANK BOOKS

Date:

Scripture for the day:

My meditative thoughts:

Date:

Scripture for the day:

My meditative thoughts:

Date:

Scripture for the day:

My meditative thoughts:

Date:

Scripture for the day:

My meditative thoughts:

Date:

Scripture for the day:

My meditative thoughts:

Date:

Scripture for the day:

My meditative thoughts:

Date:

Scripture for the day:

My meditative thoughts:

Date:

Scripture for the day:

My meditative thoughts:

Date:

Scripture for the day:

My meditative thoughts:

Date:

Scripture for the day:

My meditative thoughts:

Date:

Scripture for the day:

My meditative thoughts:

Date:

Scripture for the day:

My meditative thoughts:

Date:

Scripture for the day:

My meditative thoughts:

Date:

Scripture for the day:

My meditative thoughts:

Date:

Scripture for the day:

My meditative thoughts:

Date:

Scripture for the day:

My meditative thoughts:

Date:

Scripture for the day:

My meditative thoughts:

Date:

Scripture for the day:

My meditative thoughts:

Date:

Scripture for the day:

My meditative thoughts:

Date:

Scripture for the day:

My meditative thoughts:

Date:

Scripture for the day:

My meditative thoughts:

Date:

Scripture for the day:

My meditative thoughts:

Date:

Scripture for the day:

My meditative thoughts:

Date:

Scripture for the day:

My meditative thoughts:

Date:

Scripture for the day:

My meditative thoughts:

Date:

Scripture for the day:

My meditative thoughts:

Date:

Scripture for the day:

My meditative thoughts:

Date:

Scripture for the day:

My meditative thoughts:

Date:

Scripture for the day:

My meditative thoughts:

Date:

Scripture for the day:

My meditative thoughts:

Date:

Scripture for the day:

My meditative thoughts:

Date:

Scripture for the day:

My meditative thoughts:

Date:

Scripture for the day:

My meditative thoughts:

Date:

Scripture for the day:

My meditative thoughts:

Date:

Scripture for the day:

My meditative thoughts:

Date:

Scripture for the day:

My meditative thoughts:

Date:

Scripture for the day:

My meditative thoughts:

Date:

Scripture for the day:

My meditative thoughts:

Date:

Scripture for the day:

My meditative thoughts:

Date:

Scripture for the day:

My meditative thoughts:

Date:

Scripture for the day:

My meditative thoughts:

Date:

Scripture for the day:

My meditative thoughts:

Date:

Scripture for the day:

My meditative thoughts:

Date:

Scripture for the day:

My meditative thoughts:

Date:

Scripture for the day:

My meditative thoughts:

Date:

Scripture for the day:

My meditative thoughts:

Date:

Scripture for the day:

My meditative thoughts:

Date:

Scripture for the day:

My meditative thoughts:

Date:

Scripture for the day:

My meditative thoughts:

Date:

Scripture for the day:

My meditative thoughts:

Date:

Scripture for the day:

My meditative thoughts:

Date:

Scripture for the day:

My meditative thoughts:

Date:

Scripture for the day:

My meditative thoughts:

Date:

Scripture for the day:

My meditative thoughts:

Date:

Scripture for the day:

My meditative thoughts:

Date:

Scripture for the day:

My meditative thoughts:

Date:

Scripture for the day:

My meditative thoughts:

Date:

Scripture for the day:

My meditative thoughts:

Date:

Scripture for the day:

My meditative thoughts:

Date:

Scripture for the day:

My meditative thoughts:

Date:

Scripture for the day:

My meditative thoughts:

Date:

Scripture for the day:

My meditative thoughts:

Date:

Scripture for the day:

My meditative thoughts:

Date:

Scripture for the day:

My meditative thoughts:

Date:

Scripture for the day:

My meditative thoughts:

Date:

Scripture for the day:

My meditative thoughts:

Date:

Scripture for the day:

My meditative thoughts:

Date:

Scripture for the day:

My meditative thoughts:

Date:

Scripture for the day:

My meditative thoughts:

Date:

Scripture for the day:

My meditative thoughts:

Date:

Scripture for the day:

My meditative thoughts:

Date:

Scripture for the day:

My meditative thoughts:

Date:

Scripture for the day:

My meditative thoughts:

Date:

Scripture for the day:

My meditative thoughts:

Date:

Scripture for the day:

My meditative thoughts:

Date:

Scripture for the day:

My meditative thoughts:

Date:

Scripture for the day:

My meditative thoughts:

Date:

Scripture for the day:

My meditative thoughts:

Date:

Scripture for the day:

My meditative thoughts:

Date:

Scripture for the day:

My meditative thoughts:

Date:

Scripture for the day:

My meditative thoughts:

Date:

Scripture for the day:

My meditative thoughts:

Date:

Scripture for the day:

My meditative thoughts:

Date:

Scripture for the day:

My meditative thoughts:

Date:

Scripture for the day:

My meditative thoughts:

Date:

Scripture for the day:

My meditative thoughts:

Date:

Scripture for the day:

My meditative thoughts:

Date:

Scripture for the day:

My meditative thoughts:

Date:

Scripture for the day:

My meditative thoughts:

Date:

Scripture for the day:

My meditative thoughts:

Date:

Scripture for the day:

My meditative thoughts:

Date:

Scripture for the day:

My meditative thoughts:

Date:

Scripture for the day:

My meditative thoughts:

Date:

Scripture for the day:

My meditative thoughts:

Date:

Scripture for the day:

My meditative thoughts:

Date:

Scripture for the day:

My meditative thoughts:

Date:

Scripture for the day:

My meditative thoughts:

Date:

Scripture for the day:

My meditative thoughts:

www.ingramcontent.com/pod-product-compliance
Lightning Source LLC
Chambersburg PA
CBHW080739250626
47170CB00010B/2889
* 9 7 8 1 6 8 3 2 1 0 5 9 7 *